D0792403

Presented To

_____

By

_____

Date

_____

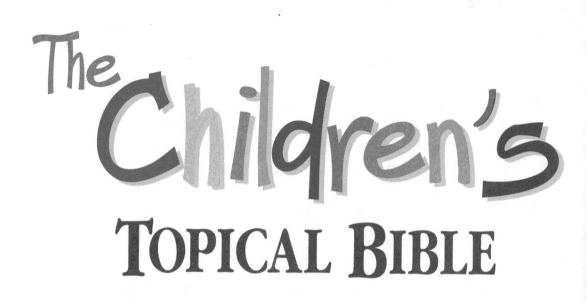

The Children's
Topical Bible

Mary Hollingsworth

Illustrated by
Jim Conaway

CONCORDIA UNIVERSITY LIBRARY
PORTLAND, OR 97211

Honor Books
Tulsa, Oklahoma

Text copyright © 1994 by Mary Hollingsworth,
Shady Oaks Studio, 4037 Scruggs at Glenview Dr., Fort Worth, TX, 76180-8821

Copyright © 1994 by Educational Publishing Concepts,
Box 665, Wheaton, IL 60189.

Published by Honor Books,
P.O. Box 55388, Tulsa, Oklahoma 74155

Scripture quotations are taken from *The International Children's Bible,
New Century Version*, copyright © 1987, 1988, 1991
by Word, Inc., Dallas, Texas 75039. Used by permission.

Printed in the United States of America.

1 2 3 4 5 6   99 98 97 96 95 94

Dedication

To my great nephew,
Austin Hansen,
with love

Contents By Topic

Topic   Page

Be A Friend 10
Be Brave 14
Be Gentle 20
Be Happy 26
Be Kind 32
Believe 38
Be Thankful 44
Do Good 50
Help 56
Learn 62
Love 68
Make Peace 74

Obey 80

Praise God 86

Pray 92

Protect God's World 98

Respect 104

Say "No" 110

Serve 116

Share 122

Sing 128

Tell Good News 134

Tell the Truth 140

Work 146

Worship 152

Index of Bible Stories 158

Dear Parents and Teachers,

As our society changes from year to year, so do some of the issues that children face. Still, the Bible is always relevant and provides answers for today's problems and issues. In truth, it is the only source of God's solutions for His children, young or old.

The Children's Topical Bible is specifically designed to help your children and students find answers to the issues and problems they face. Arranged by topic, this unique Bible story book leads children to the answers God would have them find about such troublesome topics as these: saying "no" to evil, honoring parents and teachers, ecology, obedience, respect, telling the truth and other seemingly forgotten godly attributes.

For quick reference, the topics are presented in alphabetical order and noted in bold type in the upper right corner of each page opening on which that topic is presented. If you are looking for a specific Bible story, they are indexed in alphabetical order in the back of the book, or they are noted in bold type in the upper left corner of the page(s) on which they are presented.

Two Bible stories on each topic are provided in children's language and illustrated in full-color, animated art. Interactive application questions and activities are also provided to help children move the Bible lessons from intellectual learning to life itself. These activities include topical songs to sing, prayers to pray, Scriptures to remember, things to make, riddles to solve and rhymes to read.

It is our prayer that with the help of The Children's Topical Bible, your children will begin to put God's truth and wisdom into their lives–the result is life ever after. May God bless you and the children as they learn of Him.

Honor Books

A Rooftop Adventure (Mark 2:1-12)

Jesus was teaching His followers in a house in the city of Capernaum. So many people came to hear Him preach that the house was full. No one else could get inside.

Four men brought their paralyzed friend to Jesus to be healed. They were carrying him on his sleeping mat. But they could not get through the crowd of people to Jesus.

10

Finally, the friends took the man up to the roof of the house. They made a hole in the roof above Jesus. Then down...down... down they let their friend until he was in front of Jesus.

Jesus saw that these four friends had great faith. So He said to the paralyzed man, "Stand up. Take your mat and go home." The man was healed right away! He stood up, picked up his mat, and walked

The Four Friends

out of the house. All the people were amazed!

These four wonderful friends did the best thing you can do for a friend, they took him to Jesus. You may be able to bring your friend to Jesus, too.

Remember!

A friend loves you all the time.
(Proverbs 17:17)

Ways To Be a Friend

1. What wonderful thing did the paralyzed man's friends do for him?
   (Took him to Jesus.)
2. With your art supplies draw a picture of you and your best friend. Under the picture write "Best Friends." Then mail the picture to your friend.

A Rhyme to Read

A friend in need
Needs a friend indeed,
And you can be that friend.

In all God's earth
There's nothing worth
More than a faithful friend.

A Prayer to Pray

Dear Father and Friend,
I know that You are my very best Friend of all. And I want to be Your friend, too. Please teach me how to be a faithful friend, as Jesus was to all of us.

In Jesus' name,
Amen

Attacked by a Lion! (Judges 14:5-6)

Samson was the strongest man God ever made. As a promise to God, Samson never cut his hair. His long hair meant he loved and obeyed God. As long as his hair was long, God made Samson strong.

One day Samson was walking down the road. Suddenly, a young

lion came running toward Samson. ROAR! It attacked Samson. But God's Spirit gave Samson great power. Samson killed the lion with his bare hands! It was not even hard for him to do.

Samson kept his promise to God by not cutting his hair. And God kept His promise to Samson by making him strong. God will keep His promises to you, too.

An Evil Plot (Esther 1–9)

Esther was a beautiful Jewish girl. She was chosen to be Queen of Persia. The King loved her very much.

Next to the King, Haman was the most important man in Persia. But Haman hated Jewish people, and he wanted to kill them all. Haman tricked the King into signing a law that Jewish people could be killed.

16

Esther learned about Haman's evil plan. She had to tell the King! But Esther could not go to the King unless he sent for her. If she did, he could kill her. Esther was so afraid. She prayed and did not eat for three whole days. Then she bravely went to the King.

The King was kind to Esther. He said he would give her anything

Esther

she wanted. Then Esther told him about Haman's evil plot. The King became very angry! He had Haman hanged. Then he wrote a new law to protect the Jews.

Because Esther trusted God, she was able to be very brave. If you trust in God, you can also be brave.

Remember! The Lord will honor me. I will get my strength from my God. (Isaiah 49:5d)

Ways To Be Brave

1. Pretend that you are Samson. Ask someone else to pretend to be the lion. Have a fun, play wrestling match.

   Be careful not to really hurt each other.

2. Why do you think Esther did not eat while she prayed for three days? (To have more time to pray.)

3. When are some times when you have to be brave?

   (Going to the doctor, first day of school.)

A Riddle to Guess

I am a warrior so brave and so true;
I killed a bear and a young lion, too.
I made a promise to God up above
That I would obey him and show him my love.
I am the strongest man God ever made,
As long as my hair's long enough for a braid.

Who am I?   *(Samson)*

A Prayer to Pray

Dear Lord,
I want to be brave like Queen Esther and Samson. I know they were strong because they trusted You. Please help me to trust You, too. Please help me to be brave.

In Jesus' name,
Amen

19

The King and the Kids (Matthew 19:13-15)

Jesus is the King of everything. One day He was in Judea near the Jordan River. Large crowds of people followed Jesus, and He healed them there.

Then the people began bringing their little children to Jesus. They wanted Him to touch them and pray for them.

20

Jesus' followers told the people to stop bringing the children to Jesus. They thought the children were bothering Him.

Then Jesus said, "Let the little children come to Me. Don't stop them. The kingdom of heaven belongs to people who are like these children." Then Jesus the King blessed the children before He left.

Jesus was gentle with little children, and He will be gentle with you, too.

The Gentle Shepherd (Psalm 23)

Jesus was called The Good Shepherd. He treated His followers as gently as a shepherd treats his little lambs.

Jesus gives us everything we need, just as a shepherd gives his sheep. A good shepherd leads his sheep to green pastures where they can rest. Jesus gives us peaceful rest, too.

Jesus said that believing in Him was like drinking sweet, cool water. A gentle shepherd always leads his sheep to calm water to drink.

Sheep follow closely behind their shepherd because he leads them safely down the right paths. If we follow closely behind Jesus, He will lead us safely through life.

Sheep are not afraid when they are with their shepherd. He takes

The Good Shepherd

care of them. Jesus also takes care of us.

Jesus really is like a gentle shepherd. He loves and cares for us just as a shepherd does his little lambs. We need to be gentle, too.

Remember!

Let all men see that you are gentle and kind.
(Philippians 4:5)

Ways To Be Gentle

1. If you were playing gently with a puppy, what are some
    things you would not do? (Pull its tail, pull its ears, hit it.)
2. With your crayons and paper, draw a picture of a shepherd and
    his sheep. Be sure to put in the green pasture and calm water.
3. How can you be gentle with your brother or sister? (Do not
    tease, do not hit, do not be rough.)

A Song to Sing
Tune: "London Bridge"

I am gentle with my friends,
With my friends, with my friends.
I am gentle with my friends,
Just like Jesus.

Repeat with pets, mom, dad and other
appropriate words.

A Prayer to Pray
O Lord,
    Thank You for Jesus, who is gentle
with us like a good shepherd. Please
help me to follow closely behind Him
so I can stay on the right paths. Teach
me how to be gentle with others, too.

In Jesus' name,
Amen

I Can Walk! (Acts 3:1-10)

One day Peter and John were going to the Temple to pray. They entered the city through the Beautiful Gate. Near the gate sat a man who had been crippled all his life.

The man saw Peter and John and asked them for some money. They said, "Look at us!" The man looked up, hoping for some money.

26

Peter said, "I do not have any money, but I can give you something else. By the power of Jesus Christ, stand up and walk!"

Then Peter helped the man stand up. His legs felt strong. He was healed! He was so happy. He went to the Temple with Peter and John walking, jumping and praising God. All the people were amazed.

Learning about the power of Jesus can also make you happy.

Prodigal Son

A Runaway Boy (Luke 15:11-32)

A man had two sons. The younger son wanted to leave home. So his father sadly gave him part of their money, and he left.

The younger son went to a country far away. There he spent all his money. He could not even buy food or a place to sleep.

The son took a job feeding pigs to earn some money. He was so hungry that he began eating the pigs' food. Then he thought,

"Wait a minute! Even my father's servants have a better life than this. I'll go home and ask my father to take me back as a servant."

When he was still a long way from home, his father saw him coming. The father ran down the road to meet him. He hugged and kissed him. He was so happy that his son was home.

The father gave a big party to welcome his son home. He said, "I thought my son was dead, but he is alive!" And everyone began to celebrate.

Prodigal Son

God is like this father. He is always so happy when we are at
home with Him.

Remember! Those who do right should be . . . happy
and glad. (Psalm 68:3)

Ways To Be Happy

1. Why did the crippled man jump and praise God?

    (He was happy to be well.)

2. Why was the father so happy that his son came back home? (Because he loved him so much.)

3. Why not share a tickle-and-giggle session right now?

Something to Make

Using a piece of yellow construction paper, art scissors, and a black marker, make a giant happy face. Hang the happy face in your room so you will remember that Jesus wants you to be happy.

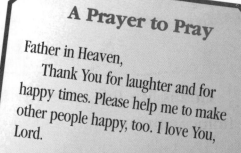

A Prayer to Pray

Father in Heaven,
    Thank You for laughter and for happy times. Please help me to make other people happy, too. I love You, Lord.

        In Jesus' name,
        Amen

Alive Again! (Luke 7:11-17)

Jesus and His followers went to a city called Nain. There He saw a funeral. A young boy had died. He was the only son of a woman whose husband had died, too. Lots of friends were walking with the woman.

When Jesus saw the sad woman, He felt very sorry for her. He said to her kindly, "Don't cry." Then He went to the coffin and touched it. The men who were carrying it stopped.

Jesus said, "Young man, I tell you, get up!" At once the young man sat up and began to talk. He was alive again!

All the people were surprised. They began praising God. Soon everyone in the whole country had heard the news about Jesus' power.

Jesus was kind to the woman who was sad. He wants us to be kind to hurting people, too.

Kindness Pays Off (Ruth 1–4)

Naomi was married and had two sons. Then her husband and sons all died. Naomi was left with her two sons' wives, Ruth and Orpah. Orpah went home to her own parents, but Ruth would not leave Naomi alone.

Ruth was very kind to Naomi. She worked hard every day picking up grain in the hot sun. They made bread to eat from the

34

grain. Everyone saw how kind Ruth was to Naomi.

Naomi's cousin Boaz also saw Ruth's kindness. He told his servants to leave extra grain in the field for her. Boaz loved Ruth and was very kind to her. Soon Boaz and Ruth were married. Then Boaz took

Ruth Is Kind

care of Ruth and Naomi.

Being kind brings happiness to everyone.

Remember!

Be kind and loving to each other.

(Ephesians 4:32)

Ways To Be Kind

1. Why was Jesus kind to the woman whose son had died? (He felt sorry for her.)

2. How was Ruth kind to Naomi? (Took care of her.)

3. With your art supplies make a get well card and send it to someone who is sick. This is a kind thing to do.

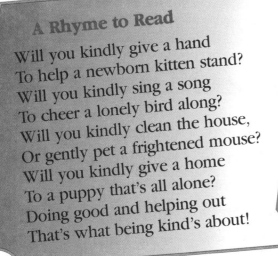

A Rhyme to Read

Will you kindly give a hand
To help a newborn kitten stand?
Will you kindly sing a song
To cheer a lonely bird along?
Will you kindly clean the house,
Or gently pet a frightened mouse?
Will you kindly give a home
To a puppy that's all alone?
Doing good and helping out
That's what being kind's about!

A Prayer to Pray

Dear God,
Many people have been kind to me, like my mom and dad, my grandmom and granddad and my teachers. I want to learn to be kind to others, too. Please help me be kind like Jesus. And thank You for being so kind to me.

In Jesus' name,
Amen

Prophet or Prince? (Matthew 16:13-20)

Jesus and His followers went to the area of Caesarea Philippi. Jesus knew that people were not sure about who He was. He asked His followers, "Who do the people say I am?"

One follower said, "Some people say You are John the Baptist."

Other followers said, "Some people say You are Elijah, Jeremiah or one of the other prophets."

Then Jesus asked them, "And who do you believe that I am?"

Simon Peter said, "You are the Christ, the Son of the living God."

Jesus smiled and said, "You are blessed, Simon. God Himself had to show you who I really am. No person could have taught you that truth. And believing that truth will unlock the secrets of My kingdom for you and the whole world."

Touched by Jesus (Matthew 8:1-4)

Jesus had been preaching to the people from a hillside. When He came down from the hill, a big crowd of people followed Him.

In the crowd was a man with a harmful skin disease. He bowed down in front of Jesus and said, "Lord, You have the power to heal

me if you want."
He really
believed Jesus
could heal him.

Jesus reached
out and touched
the man, even
though he had
the skin disease.
He said, "I want
to heal you. Be
healed!"

At once the
man's skin was
smooth and
healthy.

Believing in

A Sick Man Believes

Jesus is a very wise thing to do. It will bring you a happy life.

 Remember!

". . . I believe that Jesus Christ is the Son of God." (Acts 8:37b)

Ways To Believe

1. Ask at least three people in your family this question: "Who do you believe Jesus is?" Write their answers on a piece of paper. (Ask an adult for a little help if you need it.)
2. At the bottom of the paper, tell who you believe Jesus is.
3. Make a cross out of brown construction paper. Hang it in your room so you will always remember who Jesus is.

A Song to Sing

Tune: "This Old Man"

Jesus is God's own Son.
Ever since the world begun,
He's our Savior, Lord and
Understanding Friend
Say you'll love Him to the end.

A Prayer to Pray

Dear Father,
I believe that Jesus Christ is Your Son, and I want to be Your child, too. Help me to always believe in Jesus and to obey His Word. I love You, Father.

In the name of Jesus,
Amen

A Boy and His Lunch (John 6:1-15)

About 5,000 people followed Jesus to the other side of the lake. They wanted to see the miracles He did.

The people were hungry. So Jesus asked His followers to feed them. Andrew found a small boy who had brought his lunch. But all he had were five small loaves of barley bread and two little fish. He thought that was not enough to feed 5,000 people.

Jesus said, "Tell the people to sit down." He thanked God for the bread and gave it to the people. Then He thanked God for the fish and gave it to them too. All the people ate until they were full. All 5,000 of them!

Then Jesus' followers picked up twelve baskets of leftovers. It is amazing what can happen when we are thankful to God.

Thank You, Jesus! (Luke 17:11-19)

On His way to Jerusalem, Jesus met ten men who were sick. They had a harmful skin disease. The men called out, "Jesus! Master! Please help us!"

Jesus told the men to go and show themselves to the priests. While they were going, they were healed!

When one of the ten men saw that he was healed, he was so

happy. He ran back to Jesus. He praised God in a loud voice. Then he bowed down at Jesus' feet and thanked Him.

Do you always remember to thank God when something wonderful happens?

Remember!

"Always give thanks to God the Father for everything, in the name of our Lord Jesus Christ." (Ephesians 5:20)

Ways to Be Thankful

1. Think of someone who has done something nice for you. Call that person on the telephone and say "Thank you."

2. Jesus thanked God for the bread. When it is time for you to eat your next meal, thank God for the food you have too.

3. Write a letter to God thanking Him for all the wonderful things He does for you every day. (Ask an adult for help if you need to.)

Something to Do

Ask an adult to take you to a greeting card shop sometime. Buy a small "Thank You" card or two to give to your mom and dad. Thank them for loving you and taking care of you.

A Prayer to Pray

Dear Lord,
Thank You for the sun so bright,
Thank You for the peaceful night.
Thank You for the food we eat,
Thank You for the flowers sweet.
Thank You God for all You do.
Help me, Lord, to be like You.
Amen

The Boy King (2 Kings 22:1–23:25)

When Josiah was only eight years old he became King of Judah. For many years the people of Judah had been doing what the Lord said was wrong. God was not pleased with them.

Josiah was very young, but he did what the Lord said was right. He was a good king. And God let him rule Judah for many years.

One day Hilkiah, the high priest, found God's Book of Teachings.

It had been lost for many years. Hilkiah read God's Teachings to Josiah. King Josiah cried because Judah had not been doing what was right and good.

Then Josiah had all the false gods in Judah torn down. He lead the people back to God. Josiah did not stop doing what was right and good his whole life.

God wants us to do what is right and good all of our lives, too.

Dorcas the Do-Gooder (Acts 9:36-43)

In the city of Joppa lived a woman named Dorcas who followed Jesus. She was always doing good and helping the poor.

One day Dorcas became sick and died. Her friends put her body in a room upstairs. Then they sent for Peter, one of Jesus' followers.

When Peter came, they took him upstairs. All the poor women whose husbands had died stood around Peter. They were crying.

They showed him blouses and coats that Dorcas had made for them.

Then Peter turned to Dorcas' body and said, "Dorcas, stand up!" Right away Dorcas opened her eyes. When she saw Peter, she

Dorcas Does Good

sat up. He held out his hand and helped her up. Dorcas was alive again!

Doing good for others is just what Jesus wants us to do.

Remember!

"Learn to do good. Be fair to other people." (Isaiah 1:17)

Ways To Do Good

1. How old do you think you need to be before you start doing what God says is right and good? (Any age. Josiah was eight.)

2. Why were the women crying when Dorcas died? (They loved her; she did good things for them.)

3. Name two good things you can do for someone in your family today. Now, do them!

Something to Make

Using colored paper, make a few tickets to give away to your family or close friends. At the top of each ticket write, "Servant Ticket." In the middle write, "This ticket may be traded for one good deed by me." At the bottom of the ticket, put your name and phone number. Then hand out the tickets. When someone with a ticket wants to trade it in, do whatever they ask you to do. (Ask an adult to help you make the tickets if you need to.)

A Prayer to Pray

O Lord,

I want to be a good worker for You. Please help me learn how to do what You say is right and good. Thank You that You always give me a way to keep from doing wrong. I want to start out like Josiah and grow up to be like Dorcas.

In Jesus' name,
Amen

Please Help Me! (Mark 10:46-52)

Jesus and His followers were leaving the city of Jericho. A blind man named Bartimaeus was sitting beside the road. He heard that Jesus was walking by.

Bartimaeus shouted over and over, "Jesus, please help me!"

Jesus stopped and said, "Tell the man to come here."

Bartimaeus got up quickly and came to Jesus. Then Jesus asked,

"What do you want Me to do for you?"

The blind man said, "Teacher, I want to see again."

Jesus said, "Go. You are healed because you believed in Me." At once Bartimaeus could see again!

Jesus wants us to help people, just as He did.

Enemies! (Luke 10:30-37)

A Jewish man was going from Jerusalem to Jericho. Robbers attacked him and left him almost dead. A Jewish priest and a holy man both came by. But neither one stopped to help him.

Then a man from Samaria came along. Now, Jewish people and people from Samaria were enemies. But this Samaritan was good and kind. He felt sorry for the hurt man. So, he stopped to help the

58

Jewish man anyway.

The Samaritan bandaged the Jewish man's wounds. Then he took him to an inn and took care of him.

Before he left, the Samaritan even paid for the hurt man's room.

Good Samaritan

Then Jesus told His followers to go and help people the way the Samaritan had helped his Jewish enemy.

Remember!

Help those who are weak.
(1 Thessalonians 5:14c)

Ways To Help

1. What did Bartimaeus shout to Jesus as he walked by? ("Help me!")
2. How did the man from Samaria help the hurt Jewish man? (Bandaged his wounds, took him to an inn, took care of him, paid for his room.)
3. Think of two things you can do to help someone in your family or at school. Why not do one of those things right now?

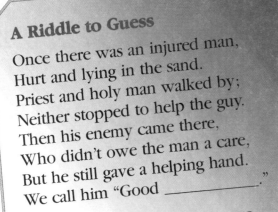

A Riddle to Guess

Once there was an injured man,
Hurt and lying in the sand.
Priest and holy man walked by;
Neither stopped to help the guy.
Then his enemy came there,
Who didn't owe the man a care,
But he still gave a helping hand.
We call him "Good _____."

Samaritan

A Prayer to Pray

Dear Father,
    I know that many people in our world need help today. Some people are hungry, some people are lonely, and some people have no coats to wear in the winter. Please show me how to help other people. I want to be like Jesus.

In His name,
Amen

Meeting at the River (Acts 16:11-15)

Paul the apostle and his friends Silas and Timothy were in Philippi. One day they walked outside the city to the river. They were looking for a quiet place to pray.

A group of women were meeting at the river. So, they all sat down and talked together.

One of the women was named Lydia. Her job was selling purple cloth—the kind that rich people wore. Lydia worshiped the true God. She listened carefully to learn what Paul taught them about Jesus.

Then Lydia and everyone who lived and worked in her house believed in Jesus. And they were all baptized. They were probably the first Christians in that part of the world!

Learning about Jesus is very important for us as well.

Lost in the Big City! (Luke 2:41-52)

When Jesus was about twelve years old, His parents took Him to Jerusalem to a big feast. The feast lasted several days. Then His parents started home with family and friends.

After traveling a whole day, Jesus' parents began looking for Him. They thought He was traveling home with His cousins or friends. But Jesus was not there!

They hurried back to Jerusalem. They looked and looked for Jesus for three whole days. They could not find Him anywhere. He was lost in the big city!

Finally they found Jesus. He was sitting in the Temple with the religious teachers. He was listening to them teach and asking them questions. He was learning everything He could about God.

Jesus as a Boy

Jesus went home with His parents to Nazareth. There He kept on learning more and more about God.

We need to learn as much about God as we can, too.

Jesus said, "Accept my work and learn from me . . . and you will find rest for your soul." (Matthew 11:29)

Ways To Learn

1. What did Lydia learn from Paul? (About Jesus.)

2. How old was Jesus when He thought learning about God was really
   important? (About twelve.)

3. What can you do to learn more about Jesus and God? (Read the Bible, go
   to Sunday school.)

A Rhyme to Read

I love to learn about God's Word
And learn about His Son,
For learning is important,
And it's really lots of fun!

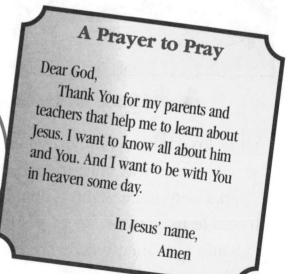

A Prayer to Pray

Dear God,
     Thank You for my parents and
teachers that help me to learn about
Jesus. I want to know all about him
and You. And I want to be with You
in heaven some day.

In Jesus' name,
Amen

A Sign from Space (Matthew 2:1-12)

God loved the people of the world so much that He sent Jesus to save us. Jesus was born to Mary in a small stable in Bethlehem.

That very same night, a brand new star glittered in the black sky! It was Jesus' star.

Some wise men who were far away saw the new star. They knew the star was a sign. It meant that God's Son had been born.

So, they began to follow the star to find Jesus.

They followed the star for a very long time. Finally it stopped right above Jesus' house. The wise men gave presents to Jesus, and they worshiped Him. Then they went back home.

Didn't God love us a lot to give up His only Son for us?

Is It a Ghost? (John 11:1-44)

Jesus had three very good friends whom He loved. They were Mary, Martha, and Lazarus. Jesus often stayed in their home.

One day Lazarus died. His sisters, Mary and Martha, were very sad. Two or three days later, Jesus came to see them. He knew that Lazarus had died.

Jesus was sad. He cried because the friend He loved had died.

Then Jesus did something wonderful! He walked out to where
Lazarus was buried. Then He shouted, "Lazarus, come out!"

Right away Lazarus came walking out of the tomb. But he was
not a ghost. He was alive again!

All the people were surprised! Mary and Martha were so happy.

Lazarus Lives Again

And that day many people believed that Jesus was the Son of God.

Do you have a friend that you love as Jesus loved Lazarus?

Jesus said, ". . . Love each other . . . as I have loved you." (John 13:34)

Ways To Love

1. How do we know that God loves us very much? (He sent Jesus to save us.)
2. Who were the three friends that Jesus loved so much? (Mary, Martha, and Lazarus)
3. Who do you love most of all?

Something to Make

Make a giant, red heart out of construction paper. Write "I love you" on it with a marker. Then give the heart to someone you love very much.

A Prayer to Pray

Dear Lord,
   Thank You for loving me so much. I love You, too. Help me to show other people Your love by being kind and good.

   In the name of Jesus,
   Amen

Joseph and His Brothers

Guess Who! (Genesis 37–45)

Joseph's brothers were very jealous of him. One day they sold him to some travelers going to Egypt. And they told their father that Joseph had died.

The travelers sold Joseph to Potiphar, an important man in Egypt. Joseph worked hard for him and was honest. After many years Joseph became ruler of Egypt.

A long time later, Joseph's brothers came to Egypt to buy food. When they found out who Joseph was, they were very afraid. They thought he would kill them. But Joseph was a good man. So, he forgave his brothers and made peace with them.

Soon Joseph's brothers and father all moved to Egypt. And they lived happily there for many years.

Making peace is always better than making trouble.

A Peace Gift (1 Samuel 25:1-42)

King David and his soldiers were hungry. They were near Nabal's herds of sheep and cattle. So, David sent a servant to ask Nabal for some food.

Nabal was a foolish man. He would not give the king any food. When David heard this, he became very angry. And he planned to kill Nabal.

Abigail was Nabal's wife. She was a very wise and beautiful woman. When she heard what Nabal had done, she decided to make peace with David. She prepared meat, bread, and fruit for his soldiers, and she took it to David herself. David was very pleased and did not kill Nabal.

Abigail and King David

Ten days later Nabal died. When David found out, he asked Abigail to become his wife. And they lived together in peace for many years.

God loves and cares for his people who work to make peace.

Remember!

"Those who work to bring peace are happy. God will call them his sons."

(Matthew 5:9)

Ways To Make Peace

1. How did Joseph make peace with his brothers who had hurt him? (He forgave them.)

2. How did Abigail make peace with King David? (She brought him a peace offering or gift.)

3. When someone hurts you, how can you make peace with them? (Forgive them, or bring them a gift of peace.)

A Riddle to Guess

I had brothers everywhere
Eleven, it's a fact.
My father gave me special care
A coat, to be exact.
My brothers sold me to a band
Of Egypt-going men,
And when in Egypt we did land,
They sold me once again.
But God turned evil into good,
And used me as his tool;
I worshiped him just as I should,
And over Egypt ruled.

Who am I? (Joseph)

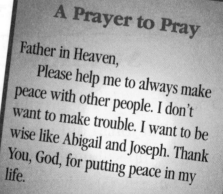

A Prayer to Pray

Father in Heaven,
Please help me to always make peace with other people. I don't want to make trouble. I want to be wise like Abigail and Joseph. Thank You, God, for putting peace in my life.

In Jesus' name,
Amen

79

Swallowed Alive! (Jonah 1–4)

God told Jonah the prophet to go to the big city of Nineveh to preach. But Jonah did not want to obey God, and he ran away. He got on a ship sailing across the sea.

BOOM! SPLASH! A terrible storm happened on the sea. The ship was about to sink! Jonah told the sailors the storm was his fault. He had not obeyed God. He told the sailors to throw him into the sea.

When they did, the storm stopped.

God sent a huge fish to swallow Jonah. He was inside the fish for three days and nights. At last God made the fish spit Jonah onto the beach.

Then Jonah went to Nineveh to preach as God had told him to do. Jonah learned that it is very important to obey God.

Snake in the Garden (Genesis 3)

God made a man named Adam and a woman named Eve. He put them in the beautiful Garden of Eden to live. God told Adam and Eve they could eat all the fruit in the garden, except one. He said, "Do not eat fruit from the tree in the middle of the garden."

One day the Devil, who looked like a snake, spoke to Eve. He told her it was all right to eat fruit from the tree in the middle of

82

the garden. He said it would make her wise like God. The fruit was pretty, and Eve was hungry. So, she disobeyed God and ate some of the fruit. Adam disobeyed and ate some, too.

God was very sad that Adam and Eve had not obeyed Him. He made them leave the beautiful garden forever.

Adam and Eve were wiser than

Adam and Eve

before. They had learned that obeying their Father was so very important. If you are wise, you will obey your parents, too.

Remember!

"Children, obey your parents the way the Lord wants. This is the right thing to do."

(Ephesians 6:1)

Ways To Obey

1. Pretend that your mom or dad has asked you to clean up your room. What should you do? (Obey) Surprise your mom or dad by cleaning your room before you are asked!

2. Ask an adult to help you read the whole story of Jonah and the big fish from Jonah 1–4 in your Bible.

3. Why did God tell Adam and Eve to leave the Garden of Eden? (They dis obeyed him.)

A Song to Sing
Tune: "Sailing, Sailing"

Sailing, sailing over the stormy sea,
Jonah ran away from God and disobeyed, you see?
It's much safer to do what God may say—
Just listen very carefully, and hurry to obey.

A Prayer To Pray

Dear God,
Thank You for Your Word that teaches me how to live and what to do. Please help me always to obey You. And please help me to obey my parents and teachers. I want You to be proud of me, Lord. I love You.
In Jesus' name,
Amen

Angels In the Sky! (Luke 2:8-15)

One night some shepherds were taking care of their sheep. Suddenly, an angel from God stood in front of them! And God's glory was shining all around them like a bright light.

The shepherds were afraid. But the angel said, "Don't be afraid. I'm bringing you some great news! The Savior of the world has been born tonight."

86

Then a large group of angels joined the first angel. All the angels were praising God. They said, "Give glory to God in heaven! And on earth let there be peace for people who please God."

Then the angels went back to heaven.

87

Trapped! (Exodus 14:5–15:21)

God's people had escaped from Egypt. But the King of Egypt was chasing them with his soldiers and chariots. When God's people came to the Red Sea, they were trapped! The sea was in front of them, and their enemies were behind them.

God told Moses to hold his walking stick out over the sea. When he did, God made a dry path through the middle of the sea. And

Moses lead the people across the sea to safety.

The King of Egypt and his soldiers followed God's people. But when they were half way through the sea on the dry path, God closed the sea over them. And they all drowned. God had saved His people.

Then Moses' sister Miriam took a tambourine in her

Miriam Praises God

hand. All the women followed her, playing tambourines and dancing. They were praising God in song. They praised Him for saving them.

We can praise God for saving us from our enemy the Devil.

Remember! "Sing about his glory! Make his praise glorious!" (Psalm 66:2)

Ways To Praise

1. Pretend that you are Miriam. Lead your family in a song of praise to God.

2. For what good news were the angels praising God? (Jesus was born.)

3. How does praising God make you feel?

A Praise Song To Sing

Tune: "This Old Man"

Praise the Lord! Praise His name!
He can heal the blind and lame.
With a song of glory,
Praise the Lord above!
Praise Him for His grace and love!

A Prayer To Pray

O Lord,
I praise You for being so wonderful! I praise You for saving us from sin. And I praise You for Your wonderful love. O God, You are the only One who deserves to be praised. I love You, Lord.

In the name of Jesus,
Amen

A Dying Man's Prayer (Luke 23:26-34)

Jesus had been arrested, but He had done nothing wrong. The soldiers led Him away. People told lies about Him to the judge. So, Jesus was found guilty.

At last, the soldiers took Jesus to a hillside. There they nailed Him to a wooden cross. Next to Jesus, two real criminals were also nailed to crosses.

92

Jesus could have been angry at the soldiers. He could have asked God to rescue Him. But He didn't. Instead, Jesus prayed for the soldiers and His enemies. He said, "Father, forgive them. They don't know what they are doing." Then He died for our sins.

To be like Jesus, we must also learn to pray for people who hurt us.

Alone With Lions! (Daniel 6)

Daniel loved and obeyed God. Three times every day he prayed to God at his open window.

Some evil men were jealous of Daniel. They wanted to kill him. They tricked King Darius into making a law that would hurt Daniel. The law said no one could pray to any god or man except King Darius.

Daniel did not obey the law. He kept on praying to the true God. So, the evil men had Daniel arrested. That night they threw Daniel into a den of hungry lions! He was sure to be eaten.

The next morning at dawn the King hurried to the lions' den. He thought Daniel would be dead. But Daniel was alive! God had sent His angel to close the lions' mouths and protect Daniel.

The King was so happy. Then he made a new law. It ordered all

Daniel and the Lions

his people to fear and respect Daniel's God.

God hears the prayers of a person who is right and good.

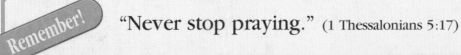

Remember! "Never stop praying." (1 Thessalonians 5:17)

Ways To Pray

1. How many times a day did Daniel pray to God? (Three) How many times a day do you pray to God?

2. Do you think Jesus' enemies were surprised to hear Him pray for them? (Yes.) Why?

3. Does God always say "Yes" to your prayers? (No.) Why not? (We have to find out what God wants for us in His Bible and be sure we are asking for the right things.)

Something to Make

Draw and cut out a pair of praying hands. Ask an adult to help you make them, if you need to. At the bottom write, "Never stop praying." Then put the praying hands on the refrigerator to remind your family to pray to God often.

A Prayer to Pray

Dear God,
Thank You for hearing me when I pray to You. I know that You will always answer my prayers in the way that is best for me. I trust You, God, to take care of me. And I pray that I will always be true to You.

In Jesus' name,
Amen

Jubilee! (Leviticus 25:8-22)

God taught His people how to take care of the world. He knew that the land needed to rest sometime. Then it would be able to grow strong crops the rest of the time.

God made a law for His people to follow. They could plant crops for six years in a row. Then they had to let the land rest for a year.

98

They also had a special year to celebrate. It was called the Year of Jubilee. When fifty years had gone by, all the slaves were set free. Land was returned to the first people who owned it. And no crops were planted. It was a year of freedom, both for the people and the land.

We must be careful to help take care of God's world today, too.

Saved from the Flood (Genesis 7–8)

God was very sad. The people He had made had become evil. They did everything God said was wrong. So, God decided to flood the earth with water.

One man was still good and did what God said was right. His name was Noah. God told Noah to build a huge boat.

Noah built the big boat exactly as God told him to do. Then God sent two of every kind of animal on earth to Noah in the boat. Finally, Noah's family got on the boat. And God closed the door.

Then God flooded the earth. But God saved Noah's family and the animals from the danger of the flood. When the flood was over, the animals built

Noah and the Big Boat

new nests and dens on the clean, new earth.

 "There will be two of every kind of bird, animal and crawling thing. They will come to you to be kept alive." (Genesis 6:20)

Ways To Protect God's World

1. How did God's people help to protect the land? (Did not plant crops every seventh year.)

2. How did Noah help to protect the animals? (Rescued them from the flood.)

3. Think of one way you can help protect the land and one way you can help protect animals that are in danger.

A Picture to Draw

Using your art supplies, draw and color a picture of Noah's big boat with the animals on it. Under the picture write "Protect God's Animals." Ask an adult to help you send the picture to your local zoo.

A Prayer to Pray

Dear God,

Thank You for our beautiful world and for all the animals. Please help me to protect the land by planting trees and flowers. And please help me to protect animals that are in danger.

In Jesus' name,
Amen

Rulers and Rules (Romans 13:1-7)

God has given special people the power to rule our country. He puts them in charge to help protect us.

That means it is important for us to respect God's chosen leaders. We must respect people like the President, senators, governors, policemen, and judges.

If we are rude to these people, or if we disobey them, it is just like being rude to God or disobeying Him. If we don't obey them, God has given them the power to punish us.

The most important reason to respect and obey God's leaders is because it is the right thing to do. That's why it's important to pray for our leaders and ask God to guide them in their jobs.

A Burning Bush! (Exodus 3:1-6)

One day Moses was taking care of some sheep. He was near Sinai, the mountain of God.

Suddenly, Moses saw a bush that was on fire. But it was not burning up. Moses thought that was very strange. So, he went closer to look at it.

Now, the angel of the Lord was inside the burning bush. As

Moses came closer the angel said, "Moses, Moses!"

Moses said, "Here I am."

Then the angel said, "Do not come any closer. Take off your sandals. You are standing on holy ground." Then Moses knew that the angel was really God Himself!

Moses took off his shoes and covered his face to show respect

Moses and the Burning Bush

for God. Then God gave Moses a very special job to help God's people.

Respect means to show honor to someone. We must always respect God, our parents and others.

Remember!
"Show respect for all people . . . Respect God. Honor the king." (1 Peter 2:17)

Ways To Show Respect

1. How did Moses show his respect for God? (Took off his shoes and covered his face.)

2. Why should you show respect for a policeman? (He is one of God's leaders.)

3. How can you show respect to your parents?

A Rhyme to Read

R-E-S-P-E-C-T,

Respectful is what I should be,
Showing honor to my mother,
Father, God, and any other.
Don't be rude or disobey;
Rather do just what they say.
God is certain to expect
Me to honor and respect.

A Prayer to Pray

Dear Father,
I know that You have chosen special leaders to rule us. Please help me to respect and honor Your leaders. Guide them in their jobs to make good decisions. Thank You for helping them, Lord.

In Jesus' name,
Amen

Run, Joseph, Run! (Genesis 39:6-23)

Joseph was in charge of Potiphar's house. No one in the house was more important than Joseph.

Potiphar's wife was evil. One day she asked Joseph to do something evil, too. But Joseph said, "No!" He would not do it. He said it was a sin against God.

Every day Potiphar's wife tried to get Joseph to sin with her. But

110

he would not do it. One day she grabbed Joseph's sleeve. But he left his coat behind. He ran away from her and the evil she wanted him to do. Joseph did exactly the right thing.

When someone tries to get you to do something wrong, always say, "No!"

Get Away From Me! (Matthew 4:1-11)

Jesus had just been baptized. Then God's Spirit lead Jesus into the desert. There He met Satan, and Satan tried to get Jesus to sin.

Jesus was very hungry because He had not eaten in forty days. Satan said, "Tell these rocks to become bread." But Jesus said, "No."

Then Satan tried to get Jesus to test God. He wanted to see if God's angels would save Jesus from falling. But Jesus said, "No."

Finally, Satan offered to give Jesus all the great things in the world. All Jesus had to do was bow down and worship Satan. But Jesus said, "No! Get away from Me, Satan. I will serve only God."

Jesus had beaten Satan. So, Satan went away and left Jesus alone. Then some angels came and took care of Jesus.

Jesus Tempted By Satan

You can beat Satan, too. When he tries to get you to do something wrong, say, "No! Get away from me, Satan." And he will leave you alone.

Give yourselves to God. Stand against the devil, and the devil will run away from you. James 4:7

Ways To Say "No"

1. Why did Joseph run away from Potiphar's wife? (She wanted him to do something wrong.)

2. How did Jesus beat Satan? (He said, "No. Get away from me.")

3. When are some times when you should say "no"? (When someone offers me drugs, when I think about stealing something, when I start to hit someone, etc.)

A Riddle to Guess

I am evil, I am mean,
I'm more clever than I seem.
I can give you many things.
Money, toys and pretty rings.
I can make the wrong seem right,
I will bring you great delight,
But when this world comes to an end,
Don't come to where I am, my friend!
Who am I?

A Prayer to Pray

Dear Lord,
It's so easy to say "yes" when someone wants me to do something wrong. Please help me learn to say "no" and run away from evil. I want to be right with You, God. I want to live with You someday.

In the name of Jesus,
Amen

115

Seven Special Servants (Acts 6:1-7)

More and more people in Jerusalem were becoming followers of Jesus. But one day an argument began.

The followers who spoke Greek were upset. Their women whose husbands had died were not getting their share of food.

The group of followers chose seven men as special servants. These men would make sure the women got their food every day.

116

This plan worked very well. And the Word of God kept reaching more and more people.

The number of Jesus' followers always grows bigger when they serve Him with love.

A King Becomes a Servant (John 13:1-17)

Jesus was the King of all the world. But He was also a gentle servant to people. He wanted His followers also to be gentle servants. So, one night He taught them an important lesson.

They were eating dinner. Jesus got up from the table. He took a towel and a bowl of water. Then He began washing and drying His followers' feet one person at a time.

When it was Peter's turn, he said, "No! You will never wash my feet." Peter did not think the King should do a servant's work.

Jesus said, "If I do not wash your feet, then you are not one of My people. A servant cannot be greater than his master. If I

119

Jesus Washes Feet

wash your feet, then you should be willing to wash others' feet."

Peter understood then that he must be a gentle servant like Jesus. And we also need to be servants like Jesus.

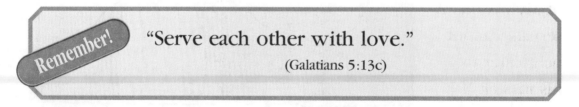

Remember!

"Serve each other with love."

(Galatians 5:13c)

Ways To Serve

1. Why were the seven special servants chosen? (To take food to the widows.)

2. Who is the greatest servant of all? (Jesus.)

3. How can you be a gentle servant like Jesus?

Something to Do

Tell your mom or dad that you want to be "Servant for a Day." Ask for special servant jobs to do around the house. Do those jobs with a big smile and lots of energy.

A Prayer to Pray

Dear Father,

Thank You for Jesus who showed us how to be servants. I want to learn how to serve others as He did. Most of all I want to serve You with my whole life. I love You, Father.

In Jesus' name,
Amen

Believers Are Blessed (Acts 4:32-36)

Those people in Jerusalem who believed in Jesus loved each other very much. The group of believers were God's church. And they all had God's Spirit living in them.

Because they loved each other, the believers shared everything they had. No person in the group was selfish with the things he owned. They all received what they needed.

Believers who owned land or houses sold them. They brought the money and gave it to the apostles. Then the apostles gave everyone the things they needed to live.

Sharing what you have with people you love makes you happy.

The Biggest Little Gift Ever (Mark 12:41-44)

One day Jesus was sitting in the Temple near the money box. He was watching people put their gifts of money in the box. Many rich people gave large gifts of money.

Then Jesus saw a poor woman come in. This woman's husband had died, and she was all alone. When she got to the money box, she put in two very small copper coins. These coins were worth

124

less than a penny.

Jesus called His followers over to Him. He taught them a lesson about sharing. He said, "This poor woman gave only two small coins. But she really gave more than all those rich people. Rich people have plenty of money. They give only what they do not need. This woman is very poor. But she has given all the money

The Widow's Mite

she had. She even gave the money she needed to buy food."

This wonderful woman gave the biggest little gift ever. She shared everything she had with God. We must share all we have with God, too. Then He will share all He has with us.

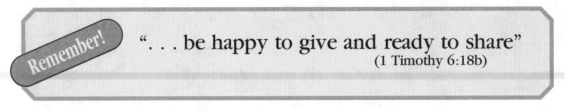

Remember!

". . . be happy to give and ready to share"
(1 Timothy 6:18b)

Ways To Share

1. What did the believers in Jerusalem share with each other? (Everything.)

2. How much did the widow share with God? (Everything.)

3. How much of what you have will you share?

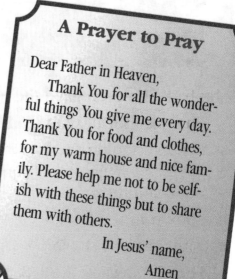

A Rhyme to Read

I will give God everything,
Everything, everything.
I will give God everything
And be happy.

I will share my clothes and shoes,
House and food, money, too.
I will share my life with you
And be happy.

A Prayer to Pray

Dear Father in Heaven,
    Thank You for all the wonderful things You give me every day. Thank You for food and clothes, for my warm house and nice family. Please help me not to be selfish with these things but to share them with others.

        In Jesus' name,
        Amen

David the Singer

The Singing King (Book of Psalms)

David was called the "sweet singer of Israel." He played a harp and wrote beautiful songs of praise to God. Many of his songs are written down in the book of Psalms. As a shepherd boy, David played and sang for his sheep.

Then he became King Saul's personal musician to help him stay calm and peaceful. At long last, David himself became King of

Israel. He was the singing king.

God tells each one of us to be singers, too. He wants us to "sing and make music in our hearts to Him," just as King David did.

Paul and Silas Sing In Jail

Earthquake! (Acts 16:16-34)

Paul and Silas traveled around the country telling people the Good News about Jesus. In the city of Philippi they got into some trouble.

Roman soldiers tore off Paul and Silas' clothes and beat them with rods over and over again. Then they threw them into jail. And they pinned down their feet between large blocks of wood so they could not escape.

About midnight Paul and Silas were praying and singing songs to God. The other prisoners were listening to them.

Rumble . . . RUMBLE . . . RUMBLE! Suddenly there was a big earthquake! The walls and ground shook. All the jail doors came flying open. The jailer thought his prisoners had escaped. And he started to kill himself.

Paul shouted, "Don't hurt yourself! We are all here."

Paul and Silas Sing In Jail

The jailer fell down before Paul and said, "What should I do to be saved?" That night the jailer and his family accepted Jesus as their Savior and Lord and were saved.

Singing is a powerful way to teach other people about Jesus!

Remember! "God is King of all the earth. So sing a song of praise to him." (Psalm 47:6)

Ways To Sing

1. Read David's most famous song in Psalm 23. Ask an adult to help, if you need to.

2. Since Paul and Silas were in a terrible jail, how could they still sing and be happy? (They believed Jesus would take care of them.)

3. What is your favorite song to sing about God?

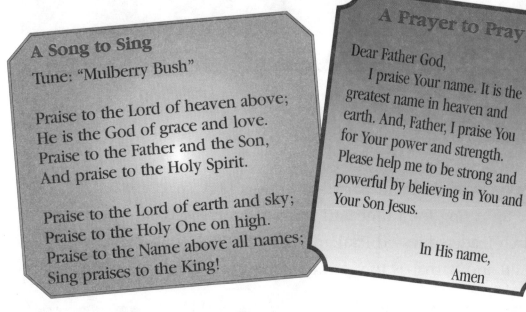

A Song to Sing

Tune: "Mulberry Bush"

Praise to the Lord of heaven above;
He is the God of grace and love.
Praise to the Father and the Son,
And praise to the Holy Spirit.

Praise to the Lord of earth and sky;
Praise to the Holy One on high.
Praise to the Name above all names;
Sing praises to the King!

A Prayer to Pray

Dear Father God,
I praise Your name. It is the greatest name in heaven and earth. And, Father, I praise You for Your power and strength. Please help me to be strong and powerful by believing in You and Your Son Jesus.

In His name,
Amen

Good News! <small>(Acts 13:1-3)</small>

In the church in Antioch were many prophets and teachers, like Paul (also called Saul) and Barnabas. They were all worshiping together.

God chose Paul and Barnabas to do a very special work. So they gave up eating for a time and prayed about the work. Then the church leaders blessed Paul and Barnabas and sent them out.

Paul and Barnabas traveled together for a long time. They told

people everywhere
they went the Good
News about Jesus.
The Good News is
how we can have
eternal life, joy, peace,
health, forgiveness and
much more. And
many people accepted
Jesus into their hearts.
Later, Paul took two
more journeys to tell
the wonderful news.

God also wants us
to tell people the
Good News about
Jesus.

Woman At the Well

He Is the Christ! (John 4:1-42)

In the country of Samaria, Jesus stopped at Jacob's well. He was tired from His long trip. So, He sat down to rest by the well.

A woman from the city of Sychar came to the well for water. Jesus asked her for a drink. The woman was surprised. Jesus was Jewish, and Jewish people were not friends with Samaritans.

Jesus and the woman talked together. He told her things about her life that no one else knew. She was amazed by what He said. Soon she knew that Jesus was God's Son.

The woman ran back to Sychar. She was so excited! She told the people there, "Come out to the well. A Man has told me everything I have ever done. I think He is the Christ!" So, the people left the town and went to see Jesus.

Jesus stayed in Samaria for two days teaching the people. Many

Woman At The Well

Samaritans became believers. The woman had brought them the Good News about Jesus. And now they were saved.

You can tell your friends the Good News about Jesus, too.

Remember! "The Good News is about God's Son, Jesus Christ our Lord." (Romans 1:3)

Ways To Tell Good News

1. Why did the apostle Paul go on three long journeys? (To tell people the Good News about Jesus.)

2. Why did the woman at the well run back to town? (To tell her friends that she had found Jesus.)

3. What are two different ways you can tell your friends the Good News about Jesus? (Invite them to Sunday school, sing them a song about Jesus, share a Bible story with them.)

Something to Make

Using your art supplies, make a small newspaper to give to a friend. On the front write "Good News" in big letters. In other places in the newspaper draw a picture of Jesus, write a short story about who Jesus is and glue a red heart that says "Jesus loves you." Think of some other things you can do in your newspaper about Jesus. When you are finished, mail the paper to someone you know who needs to learn about Jesus. Ask an adult to help, if you need to.

A Prayer to Pray

O Lord,

Thank You for the wonderful news about Jesus coming to save us. Please help me to learn how to tell my friends and others the Good News about Him. I love You, Father.

In Jesus' name,
Amen

Peter Denies Jesus

A Cock-A-Doodle Tale (Matthew 26:34-35, 69-75)

Just before Jesus was arrested, He was talking to Peter. He said, "Tonight you will say you don't know Me. You will say it three times before the rooster crows."

But Peter said, "No, I won't! I will never say that I don't know You!"

After Jesus was arrested, Peter was waiting outside. Three

different times someone asked him if he knew Jesus. Each time Peter lied and said, "No, I don't know Him."

When Peter said it the third time, he heard a rooster crow. Then he remembered what Jesus had said. And he went away and cried. He had lied about his best Friend.

Lying always brings sadness. It's better to tell the truth.

Lie or Die! (Matthew 26:57-68)

The men who arrested Jesus took Him to the house of the high priest. The teachers of the law and older Jewish leaders were there.

Many people came and told lies about Jesus. They wanted to kill Him. But the council could not find any real reason to kill Him.

Finally the high priest said, "I command You by the power of the living God to tell us the truth. Tell us, are You the Christ, the Son of

God?"

Jesus knew if He told the truth that He would be killed. But He told the truth anyway. He said, "Yes, I am."

Then the people said, "He is guilty, and He must die."

Jesus Tells the Truth

Because Jesus told the truth, we can be saved from our sin. It is always better to tell the truth, even if we get in trouble for it.

"You must stop telling lies. Tell each other the truth . . . ." (Ephesians 4:25)

Ways To Tell the Truth

1. Why was Peter so sad? (He lied about his Friend Jesus.)

2. Jesus had to die because He told the truth about who He was. Is telling the truth always easy? (No.)

3. If someone asks you if you know Jesus, what will you say?

A Picture to Draw

Draw and color a picture of the rooster Peter heard crow. Hang the picture in your room to remind you to always tell the truth.

A Prayer to Pray

Dear God,
I want to be like Jesus. Please help me to always tell the truth, even when it hurts. And please help me to tell other people that Jesus is my best Friend.

In Jesus' name,
Amen

Here Come the Ants! (Proverbs 6:6-8)

King Solomon was the wisest man who ever lived. He wrote many wise words for us to learn and live by. One story he told was about ants.

Ants are also very wise. They are not lazy, but they work hard. If you watch the ants, you can learn something important.

Ants don't have to be told what to do. They have no commander or leader. Each ant just knows what to do and does it.

In the summertime ants work hard to store up food for the winter. They gather up supplies and put them away. When winter comes they have plenty of food stored up. And they can stay out of the cold.

If we are wise, we will work hard, too. We will not be lazy.

God Makes the World (Genesis 1:1–2:3)

When time first started, God made the world and everything in it. He worked six days to make the world.

God made light and dark. He called them day and night. Then He made the sky, the dry land and the oceans.

Next God made plants, like wheat, and fruit, like bananas and apples.

The work God did the next day was to make two big lights. The biggest, brightest light He called the sun. It ruled over the day. The smaller light He called the moon. It ruled over the night.

The next day God worked at filling up the ocean with pretty swimming fish. He also made happy birds to fill the skies.

On the sixth day God made all kinds of animals, like lions, horses, dogs, and cats. He made wild animals and tame animals. Then He made the most wonderful creatures of all; He made people like you and me.

Creation

God had worked hard for six whole days. He had finished the job He began. He had made the whole world! So, on the seventh day God rested from all His work.

It is good to work hard. It is also good to rest from your work sometimes.

"While it is daytime, we must continue doing the work of the One who sent me. Night is coming, when no one can work."
(John 9:4).

Ways To Work

1. Why do the ants work so hard in summertime? (To be ready for winter.)

2. What kind of work did God do? (He made the world.)

3. What kind of jobs do you have to do at your house?

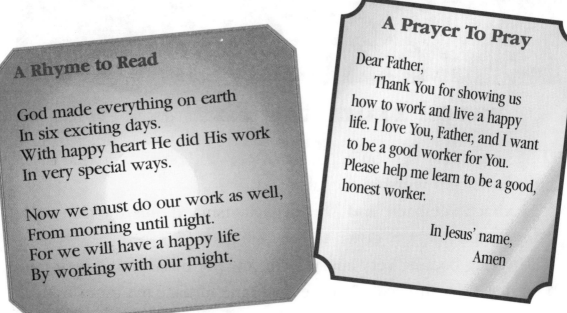

A Rhyme to Read

God made everything on earth
In six exciting days.
With happy heart He did His work
In very special ways.

Now we must do our work as well,
From morning until night.
For we will have a happy life
By working with our might.

A Prayer To Pray

Dear Father,
    Thank You for showing us
how to work and live a happy
life. I love You, Father, and I want
to be a good worker for You.
Please help me learn to be a good,
honest worker.

In Jesus' name,
Amen

Saved From the Fire! (Daniel 3:1-30)

The king of Babylon built a giant false god. He told everyone to bow down and worship the false god.

Shadrach, Meshach, and Abednego worshiped only the true God. They would not bow down to the false god.

The king became very angry. He threw the three young men into a blazing, fiery furnace. Then he made the furnace ten times hotter

152

than before.

When the king looked into the fire, he was surprised. He saw four men walking around. None of them were hurt by the fire! God had sent His angel to protect the three young men who loved Him.

The king brought the men out of the fire. Then he praised the true God of heaven!

We must worship only the true God of heaven as well.

War of the Gods (1 Kings 18:16-39)

Elijah was a powerful prophet of the true God. One time he had a contest with four hundred fifty prophets of the false god Baal. The contest was to decide whether God or Baal should be worshiped.

Baal's prophets put a bull on top of their altar. Elijah also put a bull on the altar for God.

All the prophets of Baal prayed for their god to send down fire to burn up the bull. They prayed from morning until noon. They danced around the altar, shouting, "Baal, answer us!" But nothing ever happened.

Then it was Elijah's turn. Elijah poured twelve huge jars of water on the bull and the altar. Then he prayed for God to send down fire.

SWOOSH! Fire swooped down from heaven. It licked up the water and burned up the bull. It burned up the wood and the

Elijah and Baal's Prophets

stones of the altar.

Then the people fell down to the ground. They cried and said, "The Lord is God!" They knew that only God deserves to be worshiped.

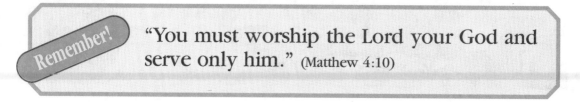

Remember!

"You must worship the Lord your God and serve only him." (Matthew 4:10)

Ways To Worship

1. How did Shadrach, Meshach, and Abednego prove that they worshiped only the true God of heaven? (They did not bow down to the false god.)

2. Why did Baal not burn up the bull on the altar to him? (He is a false god. He has no power.)

3. Who will you worship?

A Song of Worship
Tune: "Lullaby and Good Night"

God of grace, God of love,
Here I bow down before You.
You're the true God above,
And I worship only You.
Take my heart as Your own
As I bow at Your throne.
Take my heart as Your own
As I bow at Your throne.

A Prayer to Pray

Dear God,
I know that You are the one and only true God. I praise You for Your power and Your love. I worship You with all my heart. I love You, Father.

In Jesus' name,
Amen

Index of Bible Stories

Bible Story   Page

Abigail and King David 76

Adam and Eve 82

Angels Praise God 86

Ants Work Hard 146

A Sick Man Believes 40

Believers Share 122

Birth of Jesus 68

Blind Man Is Helped 56

Creation 148

Crippled Man Healed 26

Daniel and the Lions 94

David the Singer 128

Deacons Are Chosen 116

Dead Boy Lives 32

Dorcas Does Good 52

Elijah and Baal's Prophets 154
Esther 16
Four Friends. 10
King Josiah. 50
Good Samaritan. 58
Good Shepherd 22
Jesus and the Children 20
Jesus as a Boy. 64
Jesus Feeds 5,000 People 44
Jesus Prays for His Enemies. 92
Jesus Tells the Truth 142
Jesus Tempted by Satan. 112
Jesus Washes Feet 118
Jonah. 80
Joseph and His Brothers 74
Joseph Runs from Sin 110
Lazarus Lives Again. 70

Lydia Learns about Jesus 62
Miriam Praises God 88
Moses and the Burning Bush 100
Noah and the Big Boat 106
Paul and Silas Sing in Jail 130
Paul's Journeys 134
Peter Denies Jesus 140
Peter's Confession 38
Prodigal Son 28
Respect God's Leaders 98
Ruth Is Kind 34
Samson 14
Shadrach, Meshach, and Abednego 152
Ten Sick Men 46
Widow's Mite 124
Woman at the Well 136
Year of Jubilee 104

C.Lit BS 551.2 .H615 1994
Hollingsworth, Mary, 1947-
The children's topical
Bible